DARING AND DANGEROUS

SPACE EXPLORERS

ANASTASIA SUEN

Rourke Educational Media
rourkeeducationalmedia.com

Before, During, and After Reading Activities

Before Reading: Building Background Knowledge and Academic Vocabulary

"Before Reading" strategies activate prior knowledge and set a purpose for reading. Before reading a book, it is important to tap into what your child or students already know about the topic. This will help them develop their vocabulary and increase their reading comprehension.

Questions and activities to build background knowledge:

1. *Look at the cover of the book. What will this book be about?*
2. *What do you already know about the topic?*
3. *Let's study the Table of Contents. What will you learn about in the book's chapters?*
4. *What would you like to learn about this topic? Do you think you might learn about it from this book? Why or why not?*

Building Academic Vocabulary

Building academic vocabulary is critical to understanding subject content.
Assist your child or students to gain meaning of the following vocabulary words.

Content Area Vocabulary

Read the list. What do these words mean?

- *auxiliary*
- *cargo*
- *heat shield*
- *inflated*
- *lunar module*
- *mission*

During Reading: Writing Component

"During Reading" strategies help to make connections, monitor understanding, generate questions, and stay focused.

1. *While reading, write in your reading journal any questions you have or anything you do not understand.*
2. *After completing each chapter, write a summary of the chapter in your reading journal.*
3. *While reading, make connections with the text and write them in your reading journal.*
   a) Text to Self – What does this remind me of in my life? What were my feelings when I read this?
   b) Text to Text – What does this remind me of in another book I've read? How is this different from other books I've read?
   c) Text to World – What does this remind me of in the real world? Have I heard about this before? (News, current events, school, etc....)

After Reading: Comprehension and Extension Activity

"After Reading" strategies provide an opportunity to summarize, question, reflect, discuss, and respond to text. After reading the book, work on the following questions with your child or students to check their level of reading comprehension and content mastery.

1. *Describe why space exploration is dangerous. (Summarize)*
2. *Explain why you think people want to explore space. (Infer)*
3. *Why do space explorers need oxygen? (Asking Questions)*
4. *If you wanted to explore space, what would you need to do first? (Text to Self Connection)*

Extension Activity

Make a simple rocket to launch at a park or on the schoolyard. Add clay and water to an empty soda bottle made into a rocket with cardboard fins. Seal the top with a cork or a tennis ball with lots of duct tape. Wear safety goggles and launch your rocket with a bicycle pump. Make sure you have an adult's supervision. Use your phone to film the flight!

TABLE OF CONTENTS

3-2-1-Blastoff! 4
Close Calls 14
Mechanical Malfunctions 18
Hard Landings 26
Memory Game 30
Index 31
Show What You Know 31
Further Reading 31
About the Author 32

3-2-1-BLASTOFF!

Space exploration is a daring and dangerous job. *Apollo 12* was struck by lightning twice during liftoff. The astronauts had to switch to **auxiliary** power to keep going.

auxiliary (awg-ZIL-yur-ee): giving extra support; the backup

The *Soyuz T-10-1* rocket exploded during launch. Fire surrounded the men in the capsule. Workers at two mission control stations pressed a button at the same time. The rocket launched and the men survived.

Rocket Fuel

A rocket engine mixes oxygen and fuel. They explode! The hot exhaust pushes out of a nozzle. It makes the rocket move.

A teacher was going into space. Students across the country watched on live TV. Then, disaster struck. The Space Shuttle *Challenger* exploded 73 seconds after liftoff.

The entire Challenger *crew died in the explosion.*

Gus Grissom was the second *Mercury* astronaut to fly in space. After he landed in the ocean, the door blew open.

30
RESCUE
RESCUE

Tragedy struck the *Apollo 1* **mission**. The pure oxygen inside the capsule caught fire during a launch test.

mission (MISH-uhn): a specific task with which a person or a group is charged

Tragedy Yields Changes

All three *Apollo 1* astronauts died. Pure oxygen was not used again. The door was redesigned.

From left to right: Gus Grissom, Ed White II, and Roger Chaffee

CLOSE CALLS

After a ten minute spacewalk, it was time for Alexei Leonov to go back inside. But his space suit had **inflated**. It was too big to fit in the door! To get back inside, Alexei had to let oxygen out of the suit.

inflated (in-FLAY-tuhd): made bigger by pumping air into it

Pilot Ed White makes history during Gemini IV, NASA's first space walk mission.

An *Apollo 13* oxygen tank exploded! It blew a hole in the spacecraft. The crew moved into the **lunar module**. How would they get back to Earth?

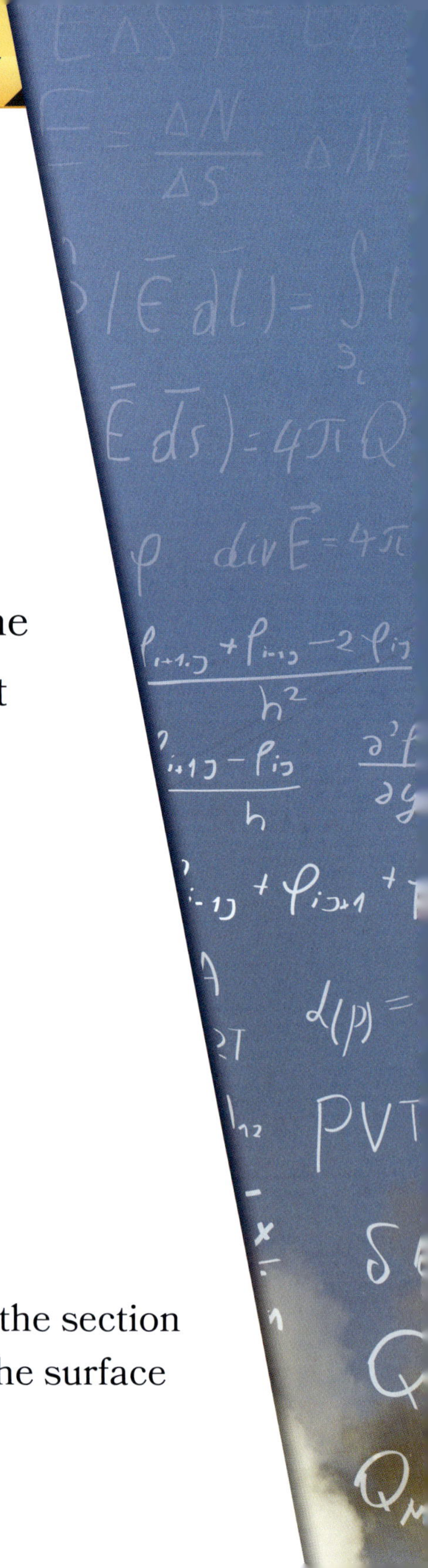

lunar module (LOO-nur MOJ-ool): the section of the spacecraft that would fly to the surface of the moon

Powered by Math

The spacecraft's computer didn't work. The crew used paper and pencil to do the math that would bring them back to Earth.

MECHANICAL MALFUNCTIONS

The first space station went into orbit in 1971. The first crew worked on *Salyut 1* for 23 days. Their *Soyuz 11* capsule lost air pressure coming home. Everyone died.

The *Mir* crew tried to land a robot **cargo** ship. It crashed into the space station. The crew had to close part of the station to stay alive.

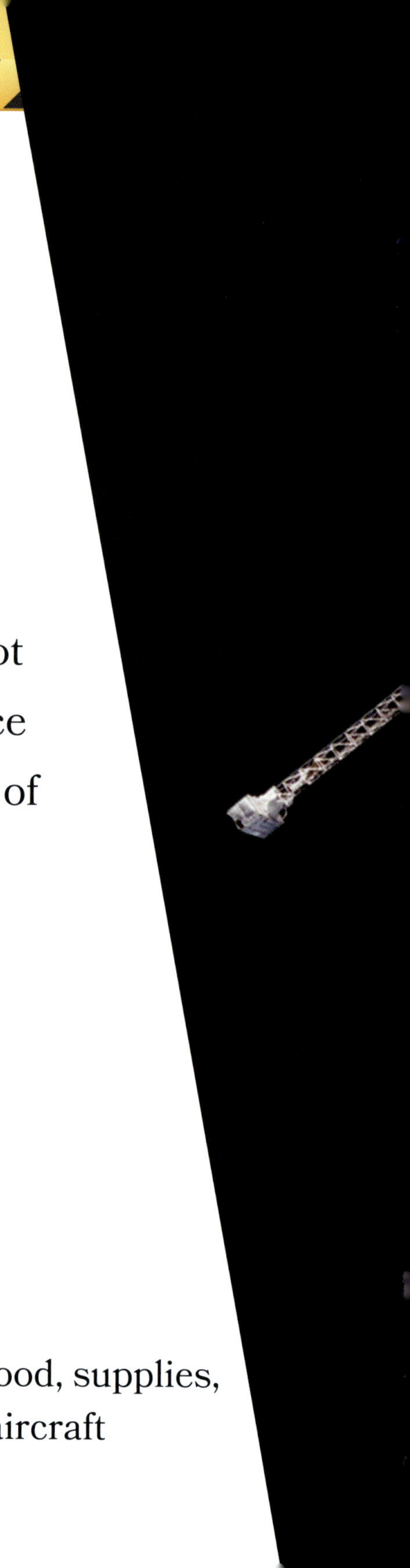

cargo (KAHR-goh): goods such as food, supplies, or other items carried by a ship or aircraft

During launch, foam came off the space shuttle *Atlantis*. It hit the **heat shield** tiles. The robot arm showed hundreds of damaged tiles. The crew thought they would die during landing.

heat shield (heet sheeld): the tiles that protect a spacecraft from catching fire as it returns to Earth

In 2003, foam fell off the space shuttle *Columbia* during launch. It hit the left wing. The shuttle caught on fire and broke into pieces during reentry.

After the entire Columbia *crew died in the accident, NASA gathered all of the shuttle debris to study what went wrong.*

HARD LANDINGS

Yuri Gagarin was the first human to orbit Earth. It took 108 minutes. As *Vostok 1* came back down, Yuri ejected! He landed with a parachute.

A model of the first Vostok rocket was built in Moscow.

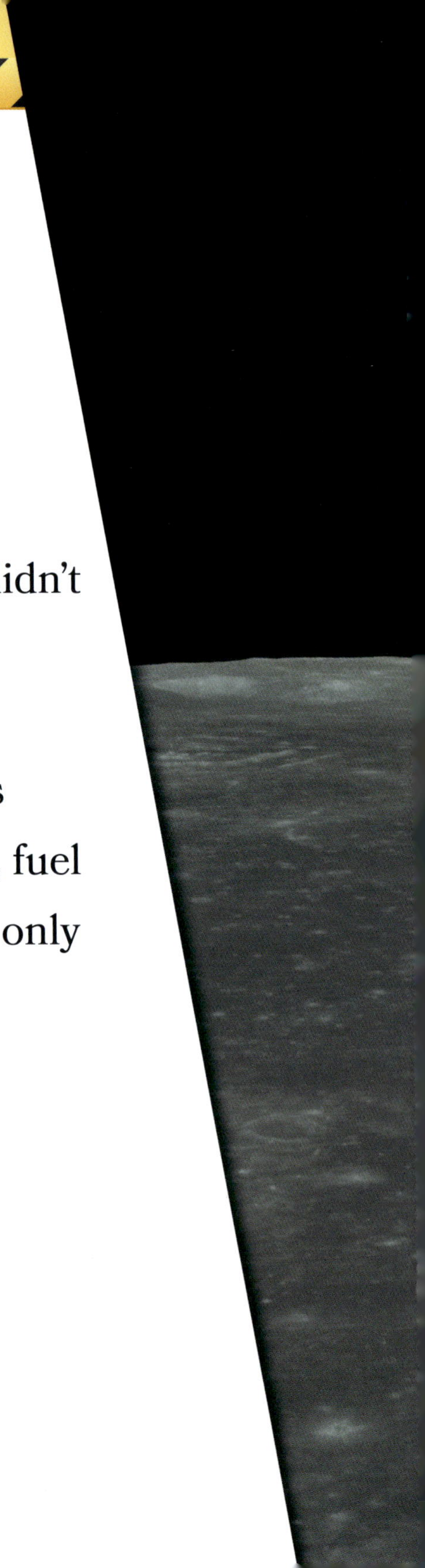

The first moon landing almost didn't happen. The *Apollo 11* computers took the crew to the wrong place. They couldn't land on boulders! As they looked for a flat place to land, fuel alarms rang. When it landed, they only had 20 seconds of fuel left.

MEMORY GAME

Can you match the image to what you read?

INDEX

Apollo 12 4
Apollo 13, 16
Atlantis 22
Challenger 8
Columbia 24
Gagarin, Yuri 26
Grissom, Gus 10, 13
Leonov, Alexei 14
space station 18, 20

SHOW WHAT YOU KNOW

1. What happened during the *Apollo 12* mission?
2. How does a rocket engine work?
3. How did the *Mir* crew survive?
4. What happened to the *Challenger* and its crew?
5. What went wrong during the first moon landing?

FURTHER READING

Jefferis, David, *Space Explorers: From Earth to Infinity*, Crabtree Publishing, 2017.

Kruesi, Liz, *Discover Space Exploration*, Lerner Publishing Group, 2016.

Yomtov, Nel, *Sailing the Solar System: The Next 100 Years of Space Exploration*, Capstone Press, 2016.

ABOUT THE AUTHOR

Anastasia Suen is the author of more than 300 books for young readers, including *Man on the Moon*, a book about the *Apollo 11* mission. She reads, writes, and edits books in her studio in Northern California.

Meet The Author!
www.meetREMauthors.com

www.rourkeeducationalmedia.com

PHOTO CREDITS: Cover, page 1, 5, 8, 9, 10, 11, 12, 13, 15, 17, 19, 20, 22, 24, 25, 29a, 29b: ©NASA; page 6_7: ©wragg; page 27: ©Stanislav Ostranitsa

Edited by: Keli Sipperley
Cover and Interior design by: Rhea Magaro-Wallace

Library of Congress PCN Data

Space Explorers / Anastasia Suen
(Daring and Dangerous)
ISBN 978-1-64369-033-9 (hard cover)
ISBN 978-1-64369-105-3 (soft cover)
ISBN 978-1-64369-180-0 (e-Book)
Library of Congress Control Number: 2018955877

Rourke Educational Media
Printed in the United States of America,
North Mankato, Minnesota